7
SECRETS
OF
ETERNAL
WEALTH

By Buck Joffrey, MD

ISBN 13: 978-1544062945
ISBN 10: 154406294X

Table Of Contents

Preface 1

Introduction 7

What people are saying about
7 Secrets of Eternal Wealth! 15

Chapter 1: Avoid Outdated and
Dangerous Paradigms 19

Chapter 2: Cash Flow Over Capital Gains
Free Yourself from the Golden Handcuffs . . 33

Chapter 3: Understand your Investments 47

Chapter 4: Invest in Real Things 55

Chapter 5: Essentials 65

Chapter 6: Momentum 71

Chapter 7: Invest in Financial Education 81

Conclusion: Wealth = Time............................89

Take Action Now 89

Disclaimer 97

Appendix 99

Preface

———∾———

"Common sense is genius dressed in its working clothes"

-Ralph Waldo Emerson

Three days after I published this book, I was pleasantly surprised to see it become an international best seller on amazon. I knew there was an audience for my message but I underestimated its size.

Emboldened by its initial success, I decided to take it on the road and promote it to television producers across the country. I saw an opportunity to carry out my mission as an evangelist for the cause of real asset cash flow investing. For the most part, my pitch was received well. Eight television producers booked me on their shows. Some didn't think it was a good fit and I didn't take it personally. One producer, however, was particularly negative about what I had to say. He said that my message was "common sense."

If my message was, indeed, common sense than my mission would be complete already. The majority of the country would not be pouring its retirement funds into stocks, bonds, and mutual funds through 401Ks. Professionals like doctors and engineers would come out of school knowing exactly how to manage their own money rather than fearfully defering to financial planners.

Let's take the concept of cash flow investing. Indeed, the concept is not difficult to understand. It is essentially the idea of buying streams of income rather than relying on appreciation. This was Robert Kiyosaki's most important message in his classic "Rich Dad Poor Dad" that he self-published in 1997. It is a simple message. Yet, Kiyosaki is the one who was the one able to explain it in such a way that it literally transformed the lives of millions of entrepreneurs. I suspect that by encapsulating his message in such elegant simplicity, Kiyosaki is responsible for more people becoming millionaires than any one human being in the history of the world. I am one of them.

My first encounter with Robert Kiyosaki's work was in an airport in Puerto Vallarta, Mexico on the way home from my honeymoon. I needed a book for the flight and I grabbed something called "The Cashflow Quandrant" off the bookshelf of a dingy little airport book-store. I had no idea what it was about but felt like I should read something about money now that I anticipated actually having some. I had just finished my surgical training a couple of weeks earlier and was anticipating a significant jump in income.

Little did I know the profound effect that little purple book would have on me. I had spent the last several years preparing for a life as an academic surgeon. That book inspired me to become and entrepreneur and would define the pivot point for the rest of my life. When I look back at what Kiyosaki was saying in that book, it all seems like "common sense" now but it was anything but that when I was a young surgeon finishing residency training. Robert Kiyosaki's genius is the ability to take complex concepts that you learn over time as an entrepreneur and investor and distil them into simple but elegant concepts. That is "genius dressed up in work clothes."

Now, I am not a genius like Robert Kiyosaki yet my mission is similar to his. For many years I took his message and ran with it. What I realized was that I had the mindset but I still needed to develop my own brand as an entrepreneur and investor. As a high paid professional who had significant earning potential as a W2 employee, I had to figure out how to implement some of these concepts into my own life. There was no road map for how to do that for someone like me. So, I did what every successful person does, I learned by trying, failing, and trying again---the proverbial "school of hard knocks." Over time, I taught myself everything I could about money, the economy and what fit in with my own personal investing philosophy.

This book is my own modest attempt at giving back a little bit what I have learned in hopes that perhaps it sparks something inside of someone the way Robert Kiyosaki sparked something inside of me and changed my life.

I hope you enjoy this book and if you want to dive deeper into the weeds, listen to my show, Wealth Formula Podcast available on itunes, sticher, youtube, google play, and I Heart Radio. You can also access more content at www.WealthFormula.com.

- Buck Joffrey, MD
February 11, 2017
Chicago, IL

Introduction

———⚬———

*Two roads diverged in a wood,
and I — I took the one less traveled by,
And that has made all the difference.*

-Robert Frost

———⚬———

I am a physician by training—a head and neck surgeon and plastic surgeon to be specific—and this book prescribes my seven secrets for financial success. You might be thinking to yourself, "Why in the world would I turn to a doctor for advice about money instead of a financial advisor?" After all, doctors are notoriously bad with money, right?

I will not dispute that stereotype. Many doctors are highly educated but financially illiterate. As highly paid professionals who have spent most of their lives as "A" students learning a specialized trade, most never got a crash course in how to handle a big influx of money. Professional schools don't spend much time teaching their students about money, and as a result, many go from being broke one day to earning a six-figure income the next, with very little direction on what to do with it. This scenario is not all that different from a blue-collar worker who unexpectedly wins the lottery.

The sudden influx of money is a foreign sensation. To remedy that discomfort, most will immediately turn to the saving grace of a financial advisor. Financial advisors who, by the way, do not take the Hippocratic oath then recommend a typical portfolio of stocks, bonds, and mutual funds. Problem solved, right? I am here to tell you that, in fact, that is where the problem actually begins. This traditional paradigm of personal money management will invariably lead to an epidemic of highly paid professionals dying broke a generation from now. I don't make this prediction flippantly. I do so because I have "done the math."

So who am I? I'm a surgeon that finished training in 2008 when a lot of senior physicians I knew lost 50-70 percent of their portfolio in the stock market late in their careers. My first "real job" was as a high paid facial cosmetic surgeon managed by a national company of corporate types. When I wouldn't practice the way they wanted me to, they fired me. I would be lying if I didn't tell you I was devastated. If you know me, I have a pretty tough exterior shell. I am 6'4 235 pound ex-ice hockey player turned surgical machine who has drilled through skulls and urgently ripped through necks to secure airways with virtually no change in my heart rate. But getting fired made me cry for days like a heart broken teenager.

For a hyper-successful individual like me, the A student who got into all the fancy schools, the class president, the homecoming king, you name it, this was a particularly unusual feeling. I was fired by someone who was not as smart as me and clearly lacked my pedigree. What a slap in the face. The devastation I felt was not because I wanted the job, it was because getting fired was failure and, like most A students, failure was a very foreign sensation. It was like the feeling you get as a child when you are scolded by your parents but know you can't fight back. It is the sensation of an ego being bruised.

Years later, I look back at getting fired and realize that it was one of the best things that ever happened to me. This blow to my ego taught me two very important lessons about entrepreneurship and investing. One: *Check your ego at the door.* An ego in the financial world can be lethal, and no one cares about your alma mater or your fancy titles. And two: *Never let a crisis go to waste.* The Chinese word for crisis also happens to mean opportunity, which has rung true throughout my short but successful career.

My crisis was being fired and not knowing what I would do next. I knew that I did not like being told what to do, so getting another "job" wasn't appealing. Fortunately, I had recently read Robert Kiyosaki's *Cash Flow Quadrant*, which I impulsively picked up at an airport bookstore on the way home from my honeymoon. This book single handedly changed my view on the financial world and gave me the mindset and courage to follow the road less travelled. So, with zero financial or business training, I decided to take this crisis as an opportunity to start my own business. Eighteen months later, I became a millionaire. Don't get me wrong, there were many challenges and setbacks along the way, but over the next few years, I started multiple high-revenue businesses and was making more money than I ever dreamed.

The one thing I was not going to do with all that money was put it in the stock market or hand it over to a Wall Street financial advisor only to see it evaporate in the next economic downturn. Instead, I opted to draw upon my father's success as a scrappy real estate investor, Robert Kiyosaki's wisdom, and my own business dealings to learn as much about investing money as I had learned about making money in the first place. Again, it was not easy. The financial world does not take the Hippocratic oath, but instead beckons scammers and charlatans. Initially navigating this labyrinth was costly and demoralizing. But what followed was financial success beyond what I had ever anticipated. Making 10 times more than the average doctor, I felt empowered in a new way. I will never again feel the uneasiness of financial ignorance and be at the mercy of someone else to secure my family's future.

Not only do I have financial freedom, I've also found myself with a lot more time on my hands. I drop my daughters off at school every day and can often be spotted in the neighborhood taking my youngest daughter for long walks in her stroller. Sometimes people ask, "Buck, I thought you were a doctor. Aren't you supposed to be working all the time?" or "What do you do for a living again?" The freedom I earned from taking charge of my own businesses and investments has made me an anomaly in a community of tirelessly hard-working, affluent people. Naturally, they wanted to know more about what I was doing.

My answers to these questions were usually ambiguous and not at all informative. Not because I was trying to keep something secret, I just didn't want to come across as a braggart. The truth is that in just eight years following my medical training, I went from being completely broke to having an eight figure net worth, and I now have the ability to "retire" at anytime.

This book is for those of you who want to know my "secrets."

To be clear, this book has nothing to do with skipping lattes to retirement. That's not reality. That's a scarcity mentality that will make you feel poor even if you're not, and I don't subscribe to it. This book is about creating a new framework for wealth that is both concrete and actionable. This framework minimizes the use of assumptions and throws the old paradigms into the garbage. Let's get started!

What people are saying about 7 Secrets of Eternal Wealth!

You've heard it said that investing isn't brain surgery. But imagine the insights a neurosurgeon turned active investor worth millions can give you, regardless of what you do for a living. If you're great at earning money, but have yet to master how to profitably invest it, read this book now!

Robert Helms
Host, The Real Estate Guys™
Radio Show and podcast

This is the lead in to a new world of techniques that only the rich people do and what the middle and poor class THINK is over their head. Pretty quick read but makes you think of why the heck does not everyone do this stuff.

Lane Kawaoka
Host, Simple Passive Cashflow
Seattle, WA

———————

This is a great book!!! Buck slays the sacred cows that most people believe in with aplomb. This is a must read and gift to be given to your friends and neighbors and especially young people just coming out of college. Read with an open heart and mind and then make the necessary changes to become wealthy.

Eric S. Tait, MD, MBA
Vernonville Asset Management
Houston, TX

Highly recommended! This is a great book for any investor at any level. There are a lot of practical insights and ideas contained within these pages. This is a book that you share with family and friends who you want to succeed in life.

Gino Castaneda, MD
Vascular Surgeon
Birmingham, AL

———— ~ ————

Concise, quick, and an easy read. I read it twice in 2 days after buying it. Dr. Joffrey has prescribed just the right medicine for wealth! Call this book "The Little Book That Could...... make you Rich"! Highly recommend it!

Jeff Thornton
Industrial Real Estate Investor
Dallas, TX

Chapter 1

Avoid Outdated and Dangerous Paradigms

—————◦♡◦—————

Each Day, each month, each year; One more, one thousand more, a million more investors will gradually learn the foolishness of this investment system and will start looking after themselves.

-John Bogle
Former CEO of the The Vanguard Group

A recent survey conducted by Mass Mutual, one of the largest insurance providers in the world, revealed that baby boomers' number one fear is outliving their savings. Death was number two.

Why are so many people afraid? Maybe it has something to do with the great recession of 2008. Or perhaps it stems from the dot.com crash of 2001, or one of the many other major market corrections in the last few decades. Whatever, the cause, many people feel instinctually uneasy about their finances and the future. And frankly, they should.

The middle class is at greatest risk, but highly paid professionals are not immune. We are working harder than ever to make as much as we did before, and often falling short. Doctors, for example, have seen a steady decline in real income every year for the past decade, despite rising healthcare costs. It just feels like something isn't right.

During the 1980 presidential campaign, Ronald Reagan famously asked, "Are you better off than you were 4 years ago?" His point was that you don't have to be an economist to understand the world's financial health. Sure, unemployment is better in 2017 then it was in 2008, and the economy is sluggishly expanding, but when you think about the world right now, do you think, "Happy days are here again"? If they were, would Donald Trump have been elected president of the United States? Politics aside, the rise of populist movements—from Donald Trump to BREX-IT—signify a global disapproval of the status quo. Regardless of other factors that have contributed to a revolt against the elite, James Carville would say, "It's the economy, stupid."

Many professionals who may seem financially stress free are also tightening their belts. A few years ago, I reconnected with one of my favorite professors from medical school. He is a well-known pediatrician in the area and has devoted his life to taking care of children. In addition to being a stellar practitioner of medicine, he has contributed a great deal to the research of various diseases and abnormalities in pediatrics. He has always been a quintessential academic physician.

I had not seen him for years, but when my first daughter was born, he just happened to be assigned to her first check up. A little older, he still exuded the same charm and energy that I fondly remembered, and we had the opportunity to catch up. Things had been going reasonably well. He was happy. In fact, his son had just graduated from Stanford, and he was a proud father. However, when he and his wife attended his son's commencement, they had to stay at a hotel almost an hour away from the university because they couldn't afford Palo Alto. I will never forget him saying that. The 2008 recession hurt a lot of good people who put their faith in Wall Street to manage their money while they worked hard with ethics and integrity. If Wall Street had taken care of his money the way he took care of our kids, he would have had no problem staying near the Stanford campus. Then again, Wall Street did not take the Hippocratic oath.

Indeed, Wall Street is to blame for the great recession that began in 2008. Not only was it the worst recession since 1929, but it also represents the end of a period of global financial stability that began after the end of the Great Depression and World War II. We understand this viscerally and have the evidence to prove it.

These are unparalleled financial times. Since the great recession of 2008, the U.S. economy has grown at a snail's pace, and even that has benefited the top 0.1% disproportionately. In fact, according to the McKinsey Global Institute, the next generation will be the first that is actually poorer than their parents since World War II. The vast majority of households are experiencing flat or decreasing incomes every year, and even doctors have increasing levels of financial uncertainty as healthcare reforms continue to whittle away at their pocketbooks.

Make no mistake; the United States Federal Reserve has tried very hard to jumpstart the economy with monetary policy. The problem is that the only tools at its disposal are decreasing interest rates and increasing the money supply, or in other words, printing more money.

Let's step back for a moment to review how the Federal Reserve uses monetary policy to maintain a happy financial equilibrium. When the economy is growing too quickly, and the risk of inflation is high, the Federal Reserve increases interest rates. Why? Because increasing interest rates make it more expensive to borrow money, and as a result, businesses slow their growth. It is not as easy to pay back the loans as it is when rates are low and money is "cheap," so businesses stop borrowing as much and slow down their growth. Raising interest rates also prevents asset bubbles. The easiest way to conceptualize this is if you think about buying a home. It is far cheaper to pay a mortgage on a $100,000 home at an interest rate of 1% than an interest rate of 5%. So, when interest rates are very low, home prices typically rise because the mortgage interest payments are so low and people can afford to pay more for the home itself. If the interest rates are high, on the other hand, the value of the house must come down to compensate for the extra interest the buyer will need to pay for on that higher interest mortgage. Broadly speaking, all assets—including stocks—behave this way. Prices go up when interest rates are low and prices go down when interest rates are high. The U.S. Federal Reserve tries to gauge the temperature and adjust the thermostat accordingly to keep the economy steadily growing while preventing asset bubbles and excessive inflation.

Before the Great Recession of 2008, we had never had 0% interest rates. It was an unprecedented move to rescue an economy during arguably the worst global financial crisis in history. The problem is that interest rates have been near zero for eight years as of the writing of this book, and despite that the global economy has only grown sluggishly. Some countries, like Japan, have even tried to use negative interest rates to stimulate the economy. What that means is that bank depositors actually pay to keep money in the bank. Sounds crazy, right? Well, don't be surprised if we end up seeing this practice in the U.S. in the not-too-distant future.

The other monetary policy tool that the Federal Reserve has is the ability to control the currency supply via quantitative easing or, in layman's terms, "printing money." Increasing the money supply is also supposed to jumpstart the economy. Since 2008, the Federal Reserve has increased the money supply by $3-4 trillion, an unprecedented maneuver that seems to have had little effect on economic growth.

Meanwhile, U.S. national debt has skyrocketed to nearly $20 trillion. For perspective, from 1775, when we started debting to pay for the American Revolution, up until 2000 the U.S. borrowed about $5 trillion. In the last 16 years alone, our national debt has increased 4 times as much as the last 225 years.

Put simply: We are in a big financial mess, and no one knows where we are headed—not even the elites who supposedly oversee the whole system. It's a big experiment right now, and the last thing you want to do is to use the same investment assumptions you did before 2008.

Nevertheless, the majority of responsible, well-paid professionals do what they believe is right: they try to create an investment plan that safely builds wealth and provides for their future. In order to do so, they heed the advice of "an expert"—the trusted financial advisor.

The financial advisor, in turn, presents outdated and dangerous investment paradigms that work better for paying advisor commissions than growing the investor's wealth. This cookie-cutter advice is based on a lot of assumptions. For example, advisors often give optimistic projections based on assumptions of at least 7% yield and 2% inflation per year. They also assume that social security will still be around in its current form decades from now. And finally, they assume that withdrawing 4% of your savings per year to live on after retirement will allow your money to outlive you. Keep in mind that every generation in recent history has lived longer than the one before it. Far more baby boomers will live to be 100 years old than those that preceded them. No wonder baby boomers worry about running out of money.

I don't like assumptions, and I certainly won't use them to plan my retirement—especially assumptions that were developed for a pre-2008 global economy that looks nothing like it does today.

So, why do wealth advisors keep telling you to do the same thing? Well, first of all, most of them don't know any better. Most of them aren't wealthy. It's not hard to become certified as a wealth advisor, and, almost all of them get paid commission on your investments regardless of market performance. In fact, once money leaves your hands, managers and banks tear it apart with commissions like a pack of vultures. According to Forbes, the average mutual fund costs about 3.5%. In other words, if you invest in a mutual fund, before you make any money on returns, 3.5%

vanishes to pay for fees. So, say you invested $1000, with 7% growth the first year. First, fees will deduct 3.5% off of that $1000, reducing your investment to $965. One year later, 7% growth will leave you with $1032.55, an increase of only 3.25%. Furthermore, these fees continue on an annual basis. It is not surprising then that the performance of mutual funds over the last three decades averages closer to 3-4% yield rather than the 10% wealth advisors may lead you to believe. Now, let's return to that assumption of 7% growth projected by these traditional paradigms. How is that going to happen? Remember, those fees to your wealth advisor are based not on profit, but rather the balance in your account. So if the market was completely flat for a year, mutual funds may actually *lose* over 3% of your money.

To be clear, there are administrative costs, like accounting, that do require compensation. But should they get paid if you lose money? I don't think so. Also remember that wealth advisors are not required to invest into the funds they recommend to you. What's to keep them from putting your money into things that pay higher commissions? Traditional money managers have no skin in the game. They win whether you win or lose. Wall Street is there to take your money, not to make you money.

So what's the alternative? Stash it away in savings accounts? As of today, the average interest rate on bank savings is less than 1%. Inflation, on the other hand, is over 1%. So that means whatever money you keep in a savings account is actually losing value. In the early 1980s, banks were offering up to 20% interest, so it made good financial sense to "save" it. But not anymore, which is why Robert Kiyosaki says, "savers are losers."

If you listen to my show, *Wealth Formula Podcast*, you know that I believe acceleration in inflation is imminent. We have not yet seen the true result of printing $4 trillion since 2008, but we will, and we will probably print even more before we're done. What happens if you print money? Logically, its value goes down. When the value of money goes down, that's called inflation. When I was a kid, I had to put $0.50 in the soda machine to pull out a can of Coke. Now, it's $2. That's how inflation affects your money and why you're going to "lose" it.

By now, I have likely either confused you, depressed you, or both. Cheer up! In the next several chapters, I will outline a better way to invest and to secure your future. I discuss principles that wealthy families around the world have used for hundreds of years. These are not new ideas, but for some reason, they seem to have been forgotten. In fact, these concepts have been the cornerstone of building wealth for most of history. Let's revisit them.

Chapter 2

Cash Flow Over Capital Gains Free Yourself from the Golden Handcuffs

———— ❧ ————

Investing for capital gains for retirement is like filling up a bottle of water as much as possible and then taking little sips, hoping you die of something else before you succumb to thirst.

-Buck Joffrey, MD
Wealth Formula Podcast

What I am going to provide you with is not a "get rich" formula; but it is a *wealth formula.* First, let me define wealth. I don't measure wealth in dollars. I measure wealth in time. The more time you have to do the things you want to do, the wealthier you are. If you could do all the things that you want to in life for $8,000 per month and didn't have to work for it, I would say you are wealthy. On the other hand, I know plenty of highly paid professionals, making upwards of $300,000 per year, "rich" by many people's standards, that I don't consider wealthy. Why? Because without constantly exchanging their own time for money they would, in very short order, be unable to pay their bills. This is a trap otherwise known as the "golden handcuffs." These professionals may be saving for retirement, but they are not accumulating cash flow with their investments and, therefore, must continue to trade time for money at the same hectic pace until retirement.

So how do you break free from golden handcuffs? I believe the answer begins with investing for cash flow rather than capital gains. Let me explain. Say I bought a business for $1 million. The value of my business may change depending on the economy and its perceived inherent value. There are, of course, many factors that contribute to this. However, as the business owner, I don't really care about the worth of my business day-to-day. It doesn't matter if someone thinks my business is worth $1 million or $2 million when I'm not actively trying to sell it. What matters more is the money that business is putting in my pocket every month. That money is cash flow. If I sold my business for $1.2 million, that extra $200,000 would be capital gains. And while earning capital gains sounds great, at the moment of sale that beautiful stream of income you had abruptly turns into a finite amount of cash.

When you invest in the stock market, you own a very small fraction of a company. In that case, you are hoping for capital gains, not cash flow. When the value of the company goes up, your stock price goes up, which can be very seductive, just like winning at a casino. You see that stack of chips get bigger and bigger and feel invincible until suddenly, your luck turns against you. The casino always wins.

A bull market can seduce the best of them; even my own father. Before the late 1990s, he had spent 30 years in real estate as a landlord, accumulating cash flow slowly but surely, making hundreds of thousands of dollars. My dad came to the U.S. in the 1960s on an engineering scholarship after growing up dirt poor in India. By the late 1990s, he was a millionaire living the American dream.

My dad is a smart guy—freakishly smart. I was a pretty good student too, but nothing like him. I never really asked him for help with my school work—except for once. I remember getting stumped on a calculus problem in high school and asking him for help. Just as I asked him to look at the problem, the phone rang and he began talking to a tenant about a broken garbage disposal. Meanwhile, he started writing down the calculus problem on the back of an envelope. Thirty seconds later, while still speaking to his tenant, he solved the problem that had stumped me for an hour, circled the answer, and handed me the envelope; all without missing a beat in the conversation with his tenant. It was pretty impressive and more then a little humbling. I never asked for math help again.

Nevertheless, by the late 1990s, even my brilliant father was lured into Alan Greenspan's mirage of an ever-expanding stock market. Ordinary people were buying tech stocks and becoming millionaires. When I was home for the holidays in December 1999, my dad spent most his time on the phone again. But this time, things were different. He wasn't just talking to tenants, he was talking to stock brokers, and the TV was tuned into CNBC all day. What the heck was this? My dad told me that he could make millions in the stock market, and it was a lot easier than collecting rent. He had started selling off properties to invest more of his hard-earned money in the market, specifically the tech sector. It sounded more appealing to me than being a landlord, but I still wasn't excited.

A couple months later, the tech bubble burst, and $1 trillion of the world's assets evaporated. My mom called me in a panic. My father told her that they had lost everything and were moving back to India with what little they had left! I thought she was joking, but when I called my dad, something was different; he was not his usual carefree self and, for the first time in my life, I heard fear in his voice. He lost 90% of his money in just days. All he had left were the few buildings he had not been able to sell, which would then be my parents' only source of income. I couldn't believe it. How could my father—the freakishly smart, financially savvy guy—lose millions in just a matter of a few weeks?

The answer is that no one can predict what will happen with the stock market, not even a guy who can effortlessly do complex calculus while talking on the phone. Very few people recognize when they are in the middle of a stock market bubble. If they did, there would be no such thing as an asset bubble! When the markets go up, "animal spirits" take over, and greed prevails. It's a big party. But when the bubble pops, the party's over.

Suffice it to say that I see at least two major dangers in this kind of investing for retirement.

First, publicly traded stock values are based heavily on speculation. It's sort of like betting at a casino. The value of the stock can be rather arbitrary and, as we saw in the dot. com era and in 2008, it can be highly volatile. Why did investors in 2008 lose more than half the value of their portfolios within days? That's a good question, and one that is really hard to answer. We know it started with some bank failures and a housing bubble. But what caused the ripple effect, which resulted in portfolios plummeting by 50%? Well, stock values in publicly traded stock are dependent on valuation, even more than earnings. Valuation is how the value of a business is determined. Most commonly, valuation equates to multiple times a company's profits. Say you own a bakery, and it makes $100,000 in profit per year. The value of such a business might be deemed as three times the profit. So, if you sold that bakery, you might expect to get $300,000. In the stock market, valuations are typically much higher and fluctuate day-to-day, often without reason. Today, for example, I see that Adobe Systems is trading on the New York Stock Exchange for 149 times its earnings. That's really expensive, right? It is. Very high prices coupled with relatively modest earnings of publicly traded companies is a primary reason why legendary traders, like George Soros and Jim Rogers, are all actively betting on a stock market collapse. When valuations become so inflated, there is no real science that can explain a stock's worth (although near 0 percent interest rates contributes). At this point, it's nothing better than gambling at a casino and, right now, the big players are all betting against it. Is this really the way you want to invest for your retirement?

The second major problem I see to investing in stocks is that no matter how much you save, your money is finite. Investing for capital gains for retirement is like filling up a bottle of water as much as possible and then taking little sips, hoping you die of something else before you succumb to thirst. That helps explain why so many people are terrified about outliving their money.

What is the alternative? Well, in the stock market, you could invest in dividend paying stocks. A dividend paying stock is simply a stock that you own, which shares some of its income with shareholders. For example, you can own Wells Fargo stock and also get a payment, which as of today, is around 3.2% per year. Why don't I advocate investing in dividend paying stocks? Well, first of all, the dividends are very low. In the case of Wells Fargo, if you invest $1,000, they will pay you $32 for the year. The majority of my investments yield greater than 10%, and I consider them failing if they fall below 7%. The other reason I don't like dividend stocks is that they too are exposed to a highly volatile stock market. If the market tanks even for reasons completely unrelated to the companies in which you own stock, your dividend payments may still be cut. In the case of Wells Fargo stock, that's exactly what happened, and shareholders were left with no control over the situation. This is yet another situation in which you are, once again, at the mercy of the "casino." Despite this, I believe that investing in dividend stocks is still preferable to investing for capital gains alone. That said, it is my preference to avoid the publicly traded markets all together.

In contrast to capital gains investing, the idea of investing for cash flow in the context of retirement takes a lot of mystery out of investing, and you will never have to guess how much you need to invest in order to retire. That is, if you if you ever want to retire.

Here's how retirement investing works using a cash flow approach. You identify an investment. Because real estate is the most common way people invest for cash flow, let's use that example. I have a friend who has a "turn-key" service selling and managing single- family homes in Alabama. That is code for: they deal with tenants and toilets, not you. After mortgage and expenses, the return on investment for each property is greater than 10% percent for the investor. Let's assume 15% for this exercise. These houses in Alabama are typically less than $100,000, but let's assume each home costs $100,000 for easy math. You put down 20% percent on the property, or $20,000 with a remaining mortgage of $80,000. With 15% return on investment, you would have $3,000 per year additional income. Even better, because it is real estate with a mortgage, that $3,000 per year is likely tax-free. With numbers like this, the math becomes much more predictable. As you keep investing, your monthly income increases. When that "passive" monthly income becomes enough for you to quit your job, you can retire. Remember, your ability to invest more increases over time with "raises" from your additional passive income accelerating your path to financial freedom. This example is simplified—but not by much. You can make it much more complex if you like, and grow your money even faster. That's what I like to do, but it's not a requirement. Here's the bottom line on cash flow investing--think income—that's what matters. You are not buying stocks; you are buying additional streams of income that do not require your time.

Compare the elegance and simplicity of cash flow investing to the unpredictable nature of traditional capital gains investing and it's not hard to see why it makes more sense. As I discussed, market volatility and unparalleled financial times alone make traditional stock investing as risky as gambling. Furthermore, trying to figure out how much you need to retire and not outlive your saved money is information that no financial advisor can provide. On the other hand, investing for cash flow—or buying income—means you create streams of money that you cannot out live. In my earlier example, I compared investing for capital gains to filling up a bottle of water and taking small sips in hopes that you will die of something else before you die of thirst. You will not die of thirst if you own several streams of income. The money does not run out and can be passed down to your heirs. Doesn't that sound more reassuring?

Now, you may be thinking, "Where am I going to get extra money for cash flow?" Good question. One answer is your IRA. Banks don't want you to know this, but you You can often use retirement funds to invest in things other than stocks, bonds, and mutual funds. Most people do not know this because the banks don't want you to know this. Why would they? If you don't put your money in stocks, bonds, and mutual funds (which you must purchase through banks and brokerage houses), they don't make any money pillaging all those commissions off your hard earned savings. The truth is, you can buy rental property, gold, debt, you name it...using your IRA. You can find out all about this by listening to episode #23 of *Wealth Formula Podcast*.

Now that you understand that investing for cash flow is simply buying streams of income, let's focus more on what to buy.

Chapter **3**

Understand your Investments

———~&~———

"Any intelligent fool can make things bigger, more complex, and more violent. It takes a touch of genius—and a lot of courage to move in the opposite direction."

-Ernst F. Schumacher
Economist and Former Chief Economic Advisor
to the UK National Coal Board

Complexity, in general, can be dangerous. I have training in neurosurgery, head and neck surgery, and facial plastic and reconstructive surgery. There is a lot of true complexity involved in these fields, as you might imagine. However, a given surgical operation may not be conceptually that difficult for a surgeon who has done it hundreds of times. In my personal experience, when bad things happen in hospitals, they are usually not because of the operation itself but the management of patients after complex surgery. There are often many medications to be administered, labs to be drawn, vitals to be recorded, and follow up tests to be performed. People working at hospitals do their best. The problem is that out of the thousands of things that occur on a surgical floor in a given day, it only takes one little honest mistake or oversight for a catastrophic patient outcome to occur. The system is just too complex. There are too many people and tasks involved and too many things to possibly go wrong. Hospitals are doing their best in recent years to put in safety measures to avoid these kinds of events, but they will never be able to eliminate errors completely in this world of complexity.

Complexity in the financial system is similar. There are markets like the New York Stock Exchange and the bond markets. Layered on top of those markets are secondary derivative markets. The derivative markets are the trading grounds for big banks and massive hedge funds. Because of complex entanglements between markets, the stock you own could be taken down in an avalanche by something unrelated to it. That's the short story on what happened in 2008. And if you think that the government has regulations in place to ensure it won't happen again, you are wrong. Banks are now twice as big as they were in 2008, and the derivative market has now reached the quadrillion-dollar mark. Wall Street is now more intertwined and scarier than ever. Best selling author James Rickards, one of the great macroeconomic thinkers of our time, likens our current financial system to an avalanche waiting to be unleashed. The only question is when and by which specific snowflake.

So, I will give you two pieces of advice here. First, try to stay out of the hospital as much as possible. Take care of your health and practice preventative care. Second, seriously consider whether you want your life savings to hinge on the next "too big too fail" moment that Wall Street experiences;— the likelihood of which has increased exponentially with the massive growth of the derivative market. Which reminds me, remember how the government came in and bailed out all the banks last time? When it happens next time, some of that bail-out money might not be coming from the government. It might be coming from you. If you have a money market account, just google search "bail in" and "money market account," and see what comes up. The new laws effectively say that banks now need to use their own deposits before tax payer money is used to bail out a bank. The bank deposits are your savings. So, if you're trying to protect yourself just by saving your money in the bank without investing, think again. Again, as Robert Kiyosaki says, "savers are losers". You will lose your money because interest pays less than inflation, and now, you will lose your money to help bail out your bank if it needs money like they all did in 2008.

So, now that I have you thoroughly terrified of banks and investing in the stock market, let me tell you some good news. Luckily, your money is yours, and you can invest it the way you want. While there are never guarantees in life and investing, you can minimize risk by avoiding complexity and investing only in things that you understand.

In order for me to invest in something, I need to understand it. And no one understands all the complex reasons behind market fluctuations. The evening of Donald Trump's election, markets crashed, but two days later, the stock market was at record highs. What really happened to change the value of your investments during that short period of time? We woke up both days under the same president, and the companies in your portfolio had negligible changes in their performance over those two days, but your wealth fluctuated massively. I don't understand these fluctuations in the stock market, so I won't invest in it.

Here is my rule of thumb: stay away from Wall Street. That means stay away from stocks, bonds, and mutual funds. Only invest in things that can be explained with a quick diagram on the back of an envelope. If you don't understand it or you don't believe it, don't invest in it. That may sound overly simplistic, but I have made millions relying on this rule of thumb as an investor.

This may sound very difficult to do but it's really not. There are numerous investment opportunities these days that do not require exposure to Wall Street and that can result in reliable cash flow. We already talked about turn-key investment homes. Let me give you one another example.

My friend Jorge has a great business called American Home Preservation. It's sort of a feel- good business. You see, Jorge's business buys failed mortgages from banks. A failed mortgage is when the home owner stops paying it. As you can imagine, there were *an awful lot* of these in 2008. However, there is no shortage of them now either. Jorge's company buys these mortgages in bulk at pennies on the dollar from the issuing bank. Then, instead of kicking people out their homes, he negotiates with them and rents the home back to the owner—with an option to buy—at a price they can afford. Because he's buying the mortgages for pennies on the dollar, the profit margin after renting these homes out is huge. But Jorge doesn't buy all these mortgages himself; he gets much of it financed through investors. In fact, you can invest as little as a few hundred bucks with Jorge, and he will give you 12% annual return on your investment issued to you as a monthly check. That's a pretty easy-to-understand model, right? I bet you could easily diagram that out on the back of an envelope. Opportunities like these are out there, and the next chapter I will share more secrets about my own investment philosophy.

Chapter 4

Invest in Real Things

———ⱬ———

" *Most people don't know whether they are investing, speculating or gambling, and to the untrained eye the activities are very similar* "

Jim Paul and Brendan Moynihan
Authors: What I Learned Losing A Million Dollars

———ⱬ———

In Roman times, an ounce of gold bought you a nice toga. In 2016, an ounce of gold will buy you a nice suit. What that tells me is that gold is real. I'm not saying that gold is a great investment, but I am saying that gold has inherent value and, over long periods of time, gold has preserved wealth better than anything else in the history of the world. If my goal was to preserve wealth over the next 1,000 years, and I had only one asset to buy, it would be gold. Gold's value does fluctuate some, but it has a pretty darn good track record in the long run when it comes to preserving wealth.

I own some physical gold and silver for this reason. It is a vehicle of wealth preservation. However, gold does not generate cash flow. It doesn't put money in my pocket every month, so I don't consider it an investment. It is money. In fact, while testifying before Congress in 1912, JP Morgan famously said, "Gold is money. Everything else is credit." The implications of this statement are beyond the scope of this book, but the general consensus of the value of gold as an asset is clear.

Stocks, bonds, and mutual funds are technically defined as assets, but they do not qualify as "real assets" by my definition. Why do I say that these financial instruments are not real assets? Let's take the example of what happened in 2008. In a very short period of time, Americans lost $7 trillion in wealth that was invested in the stock market. The assets vanished. Real assets do not vanish into thin air. When you own a rental property that someone pays you rent to live in, it does not vanish even if Lehman Brothers goes out of business. I believe in investing in real things. Specifically, I believe in investing things that you can see touch, or feel.

Let's take for example, a rental house. You can drive to that rental house, and you can see and touch it. Why? It is because it is real. People may rent that house from you, and they pay you money every month to live there. Even if Lehman Brothers collapses and the stock market crashes, they don't stop paying you rent if they still need a place to live. That's the real world. Real assets do not respond irrationally to the news of the day. Your income does not wildly fluctuate on a day-to-day basis for reasons you don't understand. In addition, because you own a real asset, the value and cash flow you receive from that asset will go up with inflation. As I mentioned earlier, I believe acceleration of inflation is inevitable. If that happens, how does that affect your rental house investment? Well, the house will increase its nominal value, and rents will go up to keep pace with inflation. Nice hedge, right? It's certainly much better than losing your money in the bank as inflation erodes its value.

Of course, like any investment, there are no guarantees. Your tenant might move out, and it might take you a month or two to find a new tenant to pay the rent. On the other hand, when there is a huge stock market correction, you lose your money, and you can't really explain why. When you own real things, you know why you've hit a pot hole, and in many cases, you can do something to remedy it. What can you do to fix a trillion-dollar loss in the stock market?

Some will argue that when you own stock, you do own something real. I would argue that owning publicly traded stock in a company is just like owning a piece of paper. When you own stock, you can't really see or touch it. You can see a number that represents its value—a value based on speculation that can vanish at any time. That is why I say stock is not a real asset.

An additional benefit, and one of the hallmarks of a real asset investment, is that it allows for a myriad of tax benefits. The government likes it when we invest in things that help our country, whereas investing in equity markets seems like just a way to make more money. If you invest in real estate, for example, the government rewards you with several tax benefits. You get to write off all of your expenses for your rental property, along with interest payments. In addition, you also qualify for depreciation benefits. The concept of depreciation has minted innumerable multimillionaires in the real estate and business world. The idea is that once you buy a rental property, it loses its value over time. In the case of residential real estate, diminishing value is spread over 27.5 years. So, using our original example, even if you made $3,000 in a year from a rental property that you used a mortgage to purchase, the IRS allows for so much depreciation that you likely won't pay any taxes on that income at all. That, my friends, is the magic of depreciation, which you will only see when you invest in real things.

Another example of a real asset investment is investing in oil and gas drilling. It has long been the U.S.'s agenda to become energy independent from the rest of the world. It certainly seems to be a good idea since most oil-rich countries don't seem to like us very much. As a result, incredible tax benefits are allowed for private investments in oil and gas companies. For example, I invested in one company that allowed me to write off 90% of my investment in the first year. Let's do the math on that one. If I invested $100,000 in this fund, I could take off nearly that much in taxable income in that same year. So, in my tax bracket, that means saving over $40,000. If you think about this in terms of return on investment (a penny saved is a penny earned),

I was able to get a 40% return in the first year simply by how much I saved on taxes. Although some of these opportunities are limited to wealthier individuals, the playing field is changing quickly.

To be clear, the more affluent still have an unfair advantage when it comes to investing in some of the world's best assets through funds and syndications. And there was a time when all of these investments required you to be an "accredited investor." The SEC defines an accredited investor as someone making upwards of $200,000 per year with a reasonable expectation to do so in the next year ($300,000 if filing jointly), or having a net worth of more than $1 million, exclusive of personal residence. While some opportunities are still reserved for accredited investors, giving them a better opportunity to amplify wealth than non-accredited investors, the world of private investments has opened up a great deal to the general public in recent years to help level the playing field. For example, several crowd-funding portals are making it easier to invest smaller sums in developments, hotels, and startup businesses every day. Even if you have only $500 per month to invest, you can now participate in various real asset funds that were previously off limits.

Furthermore, there have never been income-based restrictions on buying your own real assets. I provided the example earlier of a turn-key rental service that allows investors to own rental property without being a landlord. You can also enjoy fractional ownership in large real estate projects with no liability and all of the same tax benefits by investing with syndicators like me or other asset managers if you are qualified. My friend David Sewell sells turn-key coffee farms in Panama that are affordable to many folks, with investments starting under $10,000. Imagine that, investing in a piece of land that produces a legal, addictive drug that you can pass down to your children. Lattes are here to stay folks! Cash in now!

Opportunities for ownership in real assets are everywhere once you start looking for them. It makes more sense to invest in real assets, and I bet thinking about these tangible investments makes you realize that stock portfolios do not.

It's worth mentioning again that if you have your IRA currently tied up with paper assets, you don't have to invest in stocks, bonds, and mutual funds like the bankers would like. You can self direct your IRA with the help of people like Glen Mather over at NuView IRA. Did you know that you could invest in almost anything with IRA funds? I know one guy who makes more money through rental income in his IRA than he does from his day job!

In summary, investing should not be complicated. Make sure you invest in real things and that you understand how the investment makes money. If the investment does not meet at least these two criteria, run the other way. In the next chapter, I will further narrow down some very obvious ways of thinking about the types of real things that might make sense for your own investment portfolio.

Chapter **5**

Essentials

———⌇———

" *If you buy things you do not need,*
soon you will have to sell things
you need. "

-Warren Buffet

———⌇———

Not all real things are things we must have.
In 1954, Abraham Maslow published his book,
Motivation and Personality, in which he out-
lined a framework for human needs. It's rep-

resented with a pyramid, with basic needs at the bottom, which include physiological needs, such as food, water, and shelter. The next level up is safety. People need personal security and financial security as well as safety against accidents and illnesses. Safety is followed by love and belonging, esteem, and—at the very top—self-actualization.

My philosophy is to invest money primarily into the first two levels of Maslow's hierarchy. Why? I believe in primarily investing in things we must have, not the things we desire. No matter how tough times get, people must feed themselves and provide themselves shelter. It is no coincidence that the price of farmland has skyrocketed over the past decade. Michael Burry, a physician-turned-billionaire hedge fund manager who bet against the housing market in 2008, is now focused on investing in water rights.

I am very interested in investing in food and water and am actively looking for opportunities. David Sewell's company, International Coffee Farms, that I referenced earlier, falls under this umbrella. He offers turn-key coffee farms in Panama for investors to buy and reap the benefits of selling coffee. Perhaps investing in a legal —but addictive!— drug might classify as a basic need. After all, some of us consider caffeine a physiologic necessity! Other companies, such as Farmland LP, have created offerings for people interested in this kind of investment.

For me, the most obvious investment that fulfills the Maslow's basic rental needs is an investment in rental housing. People have to live somewhere. This can mean investing in homes, like the turn-key rentals, mobile home parks, or apartment buildings. For a variety of reasons, I prefer apartment buildings. I like the economies of scale, efficiency of management, and the opportunity to increase equity by increasing rents and decreasing expense; but that's the advanced course. If you want to learn more, listen to my *Wealth Formula Podcast* or go to www.wealthformula.com. Specifically, I prefer classes B and C apartment buildings, which are working-class buildings. Class A buildings are where the fancy people live, and class D is the no-job, no-credit crowd. Classes B and C are a stable place to be. When times get tough, Class A buildings lose tenants to Bs and Cs. Class D is just too darn difficult for me to deal with, and my only big loss in real estate was on a class D building. So, in summary, residential real estate can provide you with a solid necessity of life investment where you can be relatively sure that it won't evaporate over night, unlike your money in the stock market. It will also adjust appropriately with inflation.

Energy is another requirement for us to be safe. Imagine living without energy. How would we warm our homes? How would we transport our food and ourselves? Everything in our modern world requires energy, and it is smart to invest in it. I have interests in oil and gas drilling companies because I strongly believe that we are not that close to oil independence. Furthermore, there is a finite amount of global oil, and many experts foresee an eventual scarcity that will cause oil prices to skyrocket. As we speak, oil is pretty cheap but I, for one, am not betting against it.

And it doesn't hurt that tax incentives for investing in oil drilling companies are ridiculously favorable. An accredited investor can save a great deal of money investing in this asset class in the right situation.

Solar energy is another great investment to consider. My friend Steve has a company that installs solar panels on the roofs of large buildings and earns double-digit returns for his investors. Again, this is real stuff, and it's stuff we need. In my book, that makes for an attractive investment.

Just to be clear, I'm not saying that you should never invest outside the lower tiers of Maslow's hierarchy. It's just a little bit more risky. In real estate, people have made fortunes investing in office buildings and strip malls, and if you have a lot of money and want to get involved with those things, go for it. I also know people who invest in Hollywood productions and Broadway shows that have done very well. How about investing in ATM machines or buying other people's life insurance policies? Options outside the Wall Street Paradigm are limitless. You just need to know where to find them.

Here is one approach that might make sense to you. Begin investing for cash flow using the first two levels of Maslow's hierarchy because they tend to be more stable. Once you accumulate enough recurrent cash flow to provide for your own basic needs, take a few big swings, and try to hit some homeruns. Once your essentials are covered, you have that option.

Your personal investment philosophy will change over time depending on where your finances are and your appetite for risk. Who knows? At some point, you might shift from Maslow-based investing to a seven deadly sins approach! The goal is to get to the point where you can make those decisions safely.

Chapter **6**

Momentum

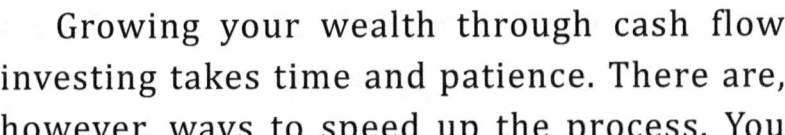

> *Focus on momentum,*
> *not perfection*

-Unknown

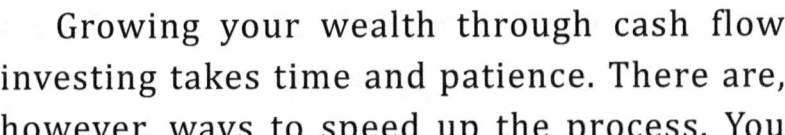

Growing your wealth through cash flow investing takes time and patience. There are, however, ways to speed up the process. You have to create momentum. In physics, momentum is defined as mass times velocity. For the purposes of this book, let's consider mass to be the amount of money you can invest annually. Velocity is how quickly you redeploy the returns on those investments to create even more cash flow.

Think of it this way, if you are making $500 per month in cash flow from a rental property and just use it to buy clothes and cars, it's not going to make you any more money. But if you immediately deploy that money into something else that creates cash flow, you keep creating more streams of income until the whole thing turns into a great big river. Velocity, the speed at which we redeploy capital, is critical in amplifying wealth.

You may have heard of this thing called the rule of 72. It is supposed to help you understand how various investment yields translate to the time it takes you to double your money. Seventy-two divided by your yield should tell you how long it takes you to double your money. For example, if you are getting a 9% yield on your investment, you simply divide 72/9, which gives you 8 years. So if you invest $10,000 at 9% per year, you will have $20,000 in 8 years, $40,000 in 16 years, etc. It's pretty straight forward, right? Not quite. I've heard even the shrewdest real estate gurus speak of the rule of 72, and in this context, they often misuse this formula. The rule of 72 is for compounding interest. What that means is that money generated on the investment is reinvested and generates even more returns after it is compounded. For example, let's say that you put $100,000 into a property, and get $9,000/year cash flow in return. That's 9% cash on cash return, right? It is. But letting that investment churn out 9% per year is not going to double your money in 8 years. In order to benefit from the "magic of compounding interest," you need to redeploy that income quickly so you can start making returns on the money you made as soon as possible as well. That is the concept of velocity. Financial advisors often use the phrase "magic of compounding interest" to describe the stock market. As outlined previously, the assumptions and uncertainty surrounding investments in the public equity markets at this time in history, along with exorbitant fees, make this an unattractive option. But you can create the "magic of compounding interest" yourself by simply redeploying capital quickly—you just have to have reliable real asset investments at your disposal at all times. My private accredited investor group addresses these issues as part of our wealth planning strategy. As of this writing, you can still join my private accredited investor group for no cost by going to www.wealthformula.com and verifying that you meet the definition of an accredited investor. Again, that definition is a $200,000 per year income ($300,000 if filing jointly) or a net worth of at least $1 million, excluding your personal residence.

Why do I have a special group for accredited investors? It's not because I'm trying to be an elitist. As I mentioned before, the world of private investing is opening up to everyday every day investors and is substantially better than it was a decade ago. However, the reality remains that there are still many potentially lucrative private investments that are open only to accredited investors. I will be the first to admit that it is an unfair advantage to be an accredited investor. But this book is not for people who want to accept their place in the world and say things are not fair. To me, fair is the "F word." My parents are immigrants who came to this country with nothing, and my father became a millionaire real estate investor by being scrappy, taking risks, and believing in himself. We live in the greatest country in the world, and opportunities are out there for anyone willing and able to take the American dream by the horns. Don't hate the rich—join them!

So, how do you increase the momentum of your financial growth? Let's go back to our physics equation where momentum is the product of mass and velocity. To maximize the momentum of your wealth, you must maximize both the mass and velocity of your investments. In other words, invest as much as you can and redeploy your returns as soon as possible.-

Now, if you are a high-paid professional, congratulations! You already have substantial mass. You might be able to invest 20% of your paycheck each month. You are already in a great position, and all you need to do is deploy your capital wisely and efficiently.

But if you barely have enough money to pay the bills, then you've got a bigger challenge ahead, and the only way out is through entrepreneurship. I mentioned my father previously. He is a classic rags-to-riches example that you often see in immigrants. They come from places without safety nets and without the rule of law to protect them. When they come to the U.S. hoping for better lives, they become like a kid in candy store. Successful entrepreneurs often see our country through a similar lens; they see it as a land of limitless possibility.

If you don't have money to invest, the first thing you have to do is to change your mindset, and seek out opportunities. You'll need to figure out how to create money that you can invest according to the principles of this book. This book is not about entrepreneurship, but I consider myself a serial entrepreneur, and the one thing that I truly believe is that with the right mindset, just about anyone can make money in our world today. Let me give you some ideas. If you are an internet savvy person, I suggest you visit Pat Flynn's www. smartpassiveincome.com and download his podcast. Pat will give you several ideas how to potentially make money on the internet. The beauty of internet businesses is that they have virtually no overhead. I personally listened to Pat's podcast for a couple of years and found his podcast on self-publishing ebooks on Amazon interesting enough to try it myself. Within a few months, I was making between $400-$700/month with books I outsourced to others on topics like the paleodiet and various other cookbooks. I chose these topics because people were buying thousands of these books every day. For reference, I discuss this experience in detail on *Wealth Formula Podcast* in an interview with Jim Kukral of Author Marketing Club (episode 026). Pat

Flynn, himself, started his blog and turned it into a seven-figure income after getting fired from his architecture job.

Another example of offline entrepreneurship that requires very little start-up costs is wholesaling homes to flippers, and there are countless sites that tell you how to do this. In short, you find homes that can be updated and flipped. But since you don't have any money, you just assign your contract over to someone who can afford it for a fee—say $3,000-5,000 at a time. It sounds too good to be true, but I know people who have done it and made money. It just takes perseverance. In fact, I know one guy who is making over $500,000 per year through his wholesaling business. He started with no money and thought of it as a way to start generating investment funds. He got so good at it that he created an entire business out of the wholesaling concept.

Even if you don't want to be an entrepreneur and start a business, you can find ways of making a little extra money now to invest, even if that means trading in more hours for dollars in the short term. For example, if you have a car, you could drive for Uber or Lyft. I guarantee you that if these services were available when I was a broke surgical resident, I would have taken advantage of them. The world is full of opportunities for people who are hungry and eager.

None of these things are going to make you a ton of money overnight, but I have seen people succeed—myself included—by simply taking the initiative to try out new things. The key is to understand that creating wealth quickly (momentum) comes from investing more money (mass) and redeploying capital as soon as possible (velocity).

Chapter 7

Invest in Financial Education

"If a man empties his purse into his head, no man can take it away from him. An investment in knowledge always pays the best interest."

-Benjamin Franklin

There is a classic scenario where a young woman has trouble with her car and goes to a mechanic. The mechanic takes a look at the car and rattles off ten things that are wrong with it. She has no idea what he's talking about but ends up agreeing to all the fixes even though her gut tells her that the mechanic might actually be taking her for a ride. Why? She has no choice. So, she ends up forking over the money, unsure about whether she got screwed over or not.

This example is no different than the young doctor who goes from a broke resident to earning a high six-figure income overnight. Just because you are book smart doesn't mean you know anything about money. I recently interviewed Rich Dad advisor, Tom Wheelwright on my show, *Wealth Formula Podcast* (episode 027). Tom said that even though doctors tend to be really smart people, they are some of the worst investors around. Why? It's because they have not taken the time to educate themselves about money and investing. Financial advisors are like sharks that smell blood around doctors. They feed on the well-to-do and advise them into the most expensive Wall Street mutual funds with the highest fees that benefit everyone in the financial industry, except the young doctor.

It boggles my mind that professional schools completely ignore financial education for their students. It is irresponsible. Knowing that a graduating student is going to go from being broke to being a top 2% wage earner overnight and not arming that student with any financial knowledge constitutes negligence in my book. Nevertheless, that's just the way the system is currently set up.

For all of you high-paid professionals out there, ask yourself this question: How much time did you study to master your professional skills so that you could make the money that you now do? Now that you make the money, shouldn't you spend at least a small fraction of that time learning how to invest it? You don't have to subscribe to my brand of investing, but you should at least take a little more time to "learn the language," so you don't end up dying broke or living with your children one day.

To emphasize, what I am suggesting is that you learn a language. Just like any specialty, the financial world has its own language, and the more proficient you are in it, the better chance you have to protect your own interests. If you choose to consult a financial advisor, you must understand the jargon and ask the right questions. Financial jargon is there to confuse you and to make you feel dumb. The goal is often for you not to ask questions out of fear of appearing stupid. Remember that most wealth advisors are paid based on fees and commissions, and they may not have your best interests at heart. That's why I don't invest with them.

If you've made your money as an entrepreneur, blind trust in financial advisors makes even less sense. Are you telling me that you are smart enough to build a profitable business only to give your hard-earned money over to someone else to invest because he or she knows more than you? It seems almost paradoxical to me, but that's what I see every day.

So how do you learn? You read, you go to seminars, and you engage with others who know more than you do. The fact that you are reading this book means you are already on the right track. I encourage you to visit my website www.wealthformula.com, which focuses on financial education and entrepreneurship for professionals. I encourage you to read all the work of Robert Kiyosaki to whom I owe a tremendous debt of gratitude for changing my own mindset about money. What he and I preach, however, is not what you will necessarily hear from mainstream financial shows like Suzie Orman. But you should learn what the mainstream financial folks have to say as well to make decisions that make sense to you. What you will find is that certain approaches to investing will philosophically resonate with you more than others. When you figure that out, you will find many ways to engage with like-minded individuals and thought leaders through seminars and field trips. Before you know it, you will start to understand your own personal investing philosophy, and you will be exposed to opportunities that fit your criteria. You will also benefit from a community of like-minded people with whom you can vet opportunities.

This is the purpose of my own investor community on www.wealthformula.com.

To be clear, the process of becoming a competent investor does not happen overnight. Like everything else, it takes time and dedication.

In the 1970s, psychologist Noel Burch described the four stages of competence. Here are the steps as I understand them:

Level 1: Unconscious incompetence. You don't know what you don't know.

Level 2: Conscious incompetence. You have insight into your own knowledge deficits and understand your current limitations.

Level 3: Conscious competence. You understand and can execute, but it is not second nature. You still have to concentrate and think things through to get them done.

Level 4: Unconscious competence. The task is second nature.

I have thought about these four stages in the context of learning new procedures as a surgical resident, an entrepreneur, and now as an investor. In all cases, the only way I got to Level 4 was to actually do the thing myself. There will be mistakes, but you learn from them, and you come back stronger and smarter.

It is virtually impossible to become highly successful and wealthy without making lots of mistakes along the way. But there are ways to limit these mistakes. Aligning yourself with a community or a mentor—or both!— is one of them. I have notoriously spent thousands of dollars over the years on coaching programs and mastermind groups. But I don't see them as expenses. In fact, I am quite sure that they have helped make me money than I ever spent. Nobody achieves greatness in a vacuum. We all need to learn from our own failure or the failures of others.

Regardless of how you approach your own situation, the bottom line is that financial education is required to do well in our world. I believe that we have tough financial times ahead over the next decade or two. These will be times when people experience extraordinary financial misery and also times when people amass great fortunes. Without a solid financial education, you will not end up on the favorable side of history.

Conclusion: Wealth = Time

Take Action Now

> *The great aim of education is not knowledge but action.*

-Herbert Spencer
19th Century English Philosopher

My first epiphany about the value of time hit me like a ton of bricks when I was in my mid-twenties. I had been accepted into an elite neurosurgery residency program. From the first day of medical school, I knew that I wanted to be a brain surgeon, and I worked like a dog in medical school to get there. I published journal articles voraciously and kissed neurosurgeons' butts like there was no tomorrow. And it all paid off. Getting into my program was statistically far more difficult than making it into the National Football League.

When I first arrived, I loved walking around the hospital with my new lab coat with my name and "Department of Neurosurgery" written beneath it. Then the night calls started. They were typically every third night or so. I'd be sleeping in my call room and my pager would go off at midnight. The emergency department would report that there was a head injury in the emergency department, and it was serious. I would be the first one down to assess the situation and, if necessary, go to the operating room with my senior staff to save a life. The rest of the night would be spent in the operating room, and the next day would come with no regard to whether I got any sleep. I would be scheduled to do four or five cases the next morning and would be expected to perform at a high level. I might not get home that evening until 7 p.m.

As much as I hated to admit it, I wasn't having any fun anymore. I liked the title, and it was good for my ego. I loved to operate and still do to this day. But I didn't like the hours! Who would right? Well, most of the other residents around me seemed to have no problem with the hours. What I came to realize was that most of them were, aside from being brilliant, adrenaline junkies. When that call came at midnight, they didn't think, "Oh no, here we go again." They thought, "Yeah baby—cracking skulls!" They would perk up as they headed to the emergency room and loved to play superman (or woman). I didn't.

It became abundantly clear to me one day when I heard a faculty member say to a senior fellow, "There are two kinds of neurosurgeons. Good ones—and those with hobbies." I didn't have a lot of hobbies, but I knew what the take home message was and when I looked around me, it was even more abundantly clear. In medical school, my neurosurgery department had more than a 100% divorce rate. Figure that one out. The chairman was rumored to have divorced more than one former Miss Texas! Don't get me wrong. These are not bad people. They are extraordinary people. Beyond the intellect to climb the neurosurgical mountain, they have superhuman physical and mental stamina, perseverance, but more often then not, no lives outside of neurosurgery. That wasn't going to be me. I wanted a life.

Although I hadn't met my wife yet, I knew I wanted to have a family one day. I wanted kids and friends to spend time with after work. I wanted to watch football on Sundays without the weight of knowing I was one phone call away from either saving someone from a brain hemorrhage or being too late to save a life. So, as hard as it was for me to change my identity and swallow my ego, I took action. I transferred to another surgical specialty that would allow me to operate and take care of patients, but still maintain a good quality of life.

I have so many friends who complain about how much they work and how much they miss their kids. It is as devastating as it is common; people with high-powered careers, prominence in their field, a nice fat paycheck each month, and a slowly growing mutual fund portfolio also have an overwhelming sense of being "shackled" to their jobs with golden handcuffs. How else would they be able to pay for the big mortgage, the fancy car payments, and the elite private-school educations for their children? These are the people that should use the secrets outlined in this book: smart, educated professionals who feel trapped in their jobs and imprisoned by a lifestyle that does not permit them the freedom to see their kids tucked into bed each night, take a leisurely vacation in the summer, or simply relax knowing the mortgage will be paid even if they suddenly get sick and need to take some time off of work.

One friend—let's call her Samantha—comes to mind. She was one of the most brilliant minds of my medical school class: always the high scorer on exams, always understood anatomy the most thoroughly. She was a rockstar. Nobody was surprised when she landed a job at the most prestigious practice in her discipline after we graduated from residency. Five years into being a partner in her practice, however, the hours of the job were really getting to her. She and her husband had had a son, and while she did not want to give up her medical career, she didn't like the feeling that she was missing so much of his babyhood so she could stay relevant at work. Most of her paycheck was going to high-quality childcare and her 401k. She was strung out, and constantly complained to me about how much she worked. The ideas in this book are for workaholics like Samantha—trading their time for money, being hard-working, responsible professionals, yet desperately seeking a way out of the golden handcuffs. Here is my prescription: Samantha should start learning about investing her hard money for cash flow. She should focus on trying to "buy passive income" that will allow her money to work for her. Over time, she will be able to work less as her residual checks start replacing overtime at the office. She should do this by first educating herself. She should read the work of Robert Kiyosaki. She should listen to podcasts like mine and get involved with likeminded communities— both on the internet and in person. From there, she can learn not only about what investments would help meet her goals, but she can also start building trust with people in her new "community." These people might be able to help her decide where she should deploy her money from their own past successful experiences. She should start with a modest investment, gain confidence, then use her momentum to build wealth and create time. The sooner she does this, the better. The time to act is now. You can lose money and always make more, but when you lose time, it's gone forever.

Disclaimer

Please note that I am not an investment advisor; this book provides my personal investment philosophy and strategies that have worked for me. You should practice due diligence on any and all future investments

Appendix

———~⌇~———

More information on things mentioned in the book:

- **Wealth Formula Podcast**: The author's podcast available on itunes, sticher, youtube, google play, and IHeartRadio. Also available at www.WealthFormula.com.

- **Investor Club**: Oriented toward Accredited Investors—those with an income of $200,000 or more ($300,000 if filing jointly) or a net worth of $1 million. The club provides a steady flow of real asset investment opportunities for accredited investors. Join at www.WealthFormula.com.

- **American Home Preservation**: Jorge Newberry's fund that buys non-performing mortgages at a discount and keeps people in their homes while providing investors with 12 percent annualized returns. www.AHPfunding.com

- **International Coffee Farms**: David Sewell's company that provides turn-key coffee farm investments in Panama. www.internationalcoffeefarms.com.

- **The Turn-key rental house provider**: Lane Kawaoka Lane@simplepassivecashflow.com. He started in Alabama but has now expanded to several other states.

- **Learning about wholesaling homes and fixing and flipping single family houses**: I never did this stuff myself but it is a viable way to create the cash (mass) you need to ultimately generate passive cash flow through other investments. A good resource is http://www.deangraziosi.com. Dean and I have mutual friends and I was lucky enough to preview a course of his for free. It is excellent material and gives you what you need. BUT...don't be one of those people who buys courses and does nothing with them.

Notes

Notes

_____

_____

_____

_____

_____

_____

_____

_____

_____

_____

_____

_____

_____

_____

_____

_____

_____

_____

Notes

Notes

Notes

www.ingramcontent.com/pod-product-compliance
Lightning Source LLC
Chambersburg PA
CBHW051727170526
45167CB00002B/828